CRYPTOCURRENCIES AND DIGITAL ASSETS REGULATION

VOLUME 2, ISSUE 1 OF BRAIN BOOSTER ARTICLES

RISHABH N. RADIA | JAY CHAUHAN AND
DHRUV J. VANJARA

Contents

Preface

"Start writing, no matter what. The water does not flow until the faucet is turned on".

-Louis L'Amour

Hundreds of students and professors are contributing their work to Brain Booster Articles, we are here to provide ample information about Law and Contemporary issues. Our aim is to provide a platform for today's generation to express their views and ideas on law and contemporary law.

Publication

This research paper is published in volume 2, issue 1 of Brain Booster Articles

Authors

Mr. Rishabh N. Radia is a 1st-year student, pursuing B.A.LL.B. at Marwadi University, Rajkot, currently doing an internship in UbAdvocate under Adv. Jeevan Prakash, AOR, Supreme Court of India. Completed internships in various NGOs like Hamari Pahchan and Tare Zameen foundation. Also got the certificate of merit in the National Client Counseling Competition organized by the Faculty of Law, Gujarat Law Society.

Mr. Jay Chauhan is a law student with critical and rational thinking, who aspires to work for the

public good. I am presently working as an Active Member of the All India Human Rights

Association which is affiliated with the United Nations. I have been an intern with NGOs such as

Hamari Pahchan, Tare Zameen Foundation, and Childo Research and Development Foundation.

Presently, Interning with AOR, Jeevan Prakash Sir, Supreme Court of India, and Working with a

law firm by the name 'Lexis and Company'.

Mr. Dhruv J. Vanjara is currently pursuing B.A.LL. B (Hons.) from the faculty of Law, Marwadi

University. Presently Interning with AOR, Jeevan Prakash, Supreme Court of India. Awarded as

the best lawyer in the National Client Counselling Competition, which was organized faculty of

Law, Gujarat Law Society. Completed his first Internship at Paryavaran Mitra NGO,

Ahmedabad.

CHAPTER ONE

Abstract

A cryptocurrency is a digital or virtual currency that is protected by encryption, due to which it is unfeasible to forge or double-spendit.[1] This essay includes recommendations for enacting legislation in India to regulate cryptocurrency. Theauthor has attempted to make recommendations based on his research of laws governing cryptocurrency regulation in other nations throughout the world. Cryptocurrencies rely on blockchain technology to function. A distributed ledger is what a blockchain is. DLT (distributed ledger technology) permits records to be kepton several computers or nodes. A node can be any blockchain user, but it takes quite a bit of computational power to run. Within the ledger, nodes check, authorize, and store data.[2]

Keywords: Cryptocurrency, Blockchain Technology, Nodes.

CHAPTER TWO

What is cryptocurrency?

Before discussing the need for regulation and/ or prohibition of cryptocurrency or virtual currencies (VCs), it is important to understand the constitution of VCs.

In the past, currencies were recommended as a way to modernize the barter system. Because they are not backed by a currency or a commodity, we call the currencies we use every day "fiat" currencies. The currency we use is a promissory note issued by the government that promises to pay the bearer the amount mentioned on the currency.

Virtual Currencies are essentially a group of binary data that is encrypted and stored to secure transaction records. Virtual Currency is not a fiat currency and is not guaranteed by the government. Virtual Currencies are built on the notion of decentralized control, and their approval is not governed by single authority. Physically, VCs do not exist. They are dispersed across a huge computer network. Unlike traditional currencies, Virtual Currencies have a finite supply. The value of a coin is specified in every ASCII computer file. For example, there's only 21 millionBitcoins[3] available. As a result, as the demand for Virtual Currencies grows, so does its value. It operates on the demand and supply principle.

Virtual Currencies also have the benefit of removing third-party merchants such as Visa or Master Card, which eliminates the need for an end user to pay commission, lowering transaction costs.

They are also unavoidable. As a result, once a transaction is completed, it cannot be altered. The VCs are kept in a virtual wallet that only a private key can access. It's like an impenetrable vault that can only be launched with the keys provided. If you lose the key, you lose access to the vault's contents.

However, one of the most visible benefits of Virtual Currencies is that they can be "mined" by a computer, which involves a process of solving arithmetic problems or algorithms that are being used to verify transaction blocks to be added to the blockchain. As previously stated, VCs are protected by blockchain, which is a huge amount of transactions. A computer can be used to authentic at these transactions and receive a cryptocurrency as are ward.

CHAPTER THREE

The need for regulation

If VCs have so many benefits, then why are the Governments sceptical of considering them as legal tender?

In a nutshell, the answer is privacy. VCs are built on highly secure blockchain technology. A wallet is associated with a private key instead of a specific person. As a result, governments have a difficult time tracing the roots of a transaction. Because Virtual currencies use pseudonyms to conduct transactions, they have the potential to be used for illegal purposes.

Another concern is that because Virtual currencies are not backed by the government or any commodity, their values can fall if the promoter of the VCs ceases trading activity. The most recent example is the Squid Game Crypto Scam, in which the promoters are estimated to havederauded an estimated $3.38 million by attracting buyers and then ceasing trading, leaving the buyers with tokens with no financial value.[4]

CHAPTER FOUR

Chequered History of VCs in India

In India, the Reserve Bank of India ("RBI") has expressed concerns about VCs and the lack of safeguards over the years. What appears to be the RBI's apprehension and reluctance manifested itself in a circular[5] issued by the Reserve Bank on April 6, 2018 ("2018 Circular") banning all entities regulated by the RBI from rendering services in connection with Virtual currencies, including maintaining accounts, registering, trading, settling, clearing, lending against virtual tokens, accepting them as collateral, opening accounts of exchanges having dealt with them, and transferring/ receiving money in accounts. This circular was later overturned by the Supreme Court in the case of Internet and Mobile Association of India v. Reserve Bank of IndiainMarch2020.[6]

It was held by the Supreme Court in the afore mentioned case that 'The position as on date is that VCs are not banned, but the trading in VCs and the functioning of VC exchanges are sent to comatose by the impugned Circular by disconnecting their lifeline namely, the interface with the regular banking sector. What is worse is that this has been done (i) despite RBI not finding anything wrong about the way in which these exchanges function and (ii) despite the fact that VCs are not banned'.

Following the Supreme Court's decision, the RBI issued a follow-up circular on May 31, 2021[7], stating that the 2018 Circular was no longer valid in light of the Supreme Court's decision and instructing entities regulated by it not to rely on it.

It is also relevant to note that the SC Garg Committee ("**Committee**") in 2019, led the charge to ban VCs, the Committee put forth its concerns regarding the ballooning of VCs in its report[8] and stated that nearly all VCs are issued abroad with huge numbers of people in India investing in them.

The report stated that, "All these cryptocurrencies have been created by non-sovereigns and are in this sense entirely private enterprises and there is noun derlying intrinsic value of these private crypto currencies due to which they lack all theat tributes of a currency."

According to the Report of the committee, VCs will not be able to function as a currency because they lack the essential characteristics of currency; it also advised the government to keep an open mind when it comes to an authorized digital currency. Both the Committee and the RBI believe that VCs pose a risk of being used for money laundering and have long been referred as volatile and risky investments by the RBI.

CHAPTER FIVE

Countries where Cryptocurrencies are legal

The Library of Congress (LOC) evaluates countries' positions on Cryptocurrency on a regular basis. It listed 103 countries whose authorities asked their financial regulatory authorities to draught legislation and priorities for financial firms addressing cryptocurrencies and their usage in anti-money laundering and counter-terrorist financing in November 2021.

The LOC also identified many countries that allow cryptocurrencies to be used. Here area few of them.

The United States

Since 2013, the Financial Crimes Enforcement Network (FinCEN) of the United States Department of Treasury has issued Bitcoin recommendations. Bitcoin is described by the Treasury as a transferable currency having a real-world equivalent or one that may be used as a substitute for proper money.[9]

A money services business is defined as any entity that manages or exchanges Bitcoin, such as crypto exchange and payment processors (MSB). As a result, an MSB is subject to the Bank Secrecy Act and must register with the United States Treasury and file reports on transactions over $10,000, including bitcoin purchases.[10]

FinCEN is also working on rules for financial as well as non-financial entities to set national priorities for bitcoin tracking and reporting. This legislation will force these organizations to disclose certain transactions and suspicious behaviour, such as banks and virtual currencies. They will be able to examine suspected financial fraud and unlawful activity using crypto currency thanks to this reporting.[11]

The European Union

Digital currencies are classified as crypto-assets by the European Union. Although it is not illegal to use Bitcoin in the EU, the European Banking

Authority, the union's currency regulator, has warned that crypto-asset activities are beyond itscontrol and continues to caution the public and businesses about the dangers ofbitcoin.[12]

In 2020, The European Commission concluded a proposition for regulation to control crypto-resources, which numerous organizations have supported inside the association. This regulation is expected to hold monetary administrative systems back from dividing and level the monetary battle ground across the EU. The commission likewise needs to guarantee people in general approaches and cansecurelyutilize cryptographic money.[13]

Canada

Canada keeps a for the most part bitcoin-accommodating position like its southern neighbour, the U.S. Bitcoin is considered to be an item by the Canada Revenue Agency (CRA) for annual expense purposes. This implies any pay from anexchange utilizing Bitcoin is seen as business pay or a capital addition and should be accounted for all thingsconsidered.[14]

Canada considers digital currency trades to be cash administration organizations. This brings them under the domain of the Proceeds of Crime (Money Laundering) and Terrorist Financing Act (Canada's variant of AML/CFT regulations).Subsequently, digital money trades need to enrol with the Financial Transactions and Reports Analysis Centre of Canada (FINTRAC), report any dubious exchanges, submit to the consistence designs, and even keep specific records.[15]

Australia

Like Canada, the Australian Taxation Office considers Bitcoin a monetary resource with esteem that can be burdened when explicit occasions happen. In the event that you exchange, trade, offer, gift, convert it to government issued money, or use Bitcoin for buys, you trigger a capital increases charge. You're additionally expected to track any exchanges you make involving Bitcoin for charge purposes.[16]

ElSalvador

El Salvador is the main country on the planet that has announced bitcoin to be lawful delicate. In June 2021, the country's Congress endorsed President NayibBukele to officially embrace bitcoin as a type of instalment.

CHAPTER SIX

The way forward

The proposed Legislation may presumably serve to introduce a standard of uniformity of understanding and bring the gov't agencies involved on the same page, while also providing security and assisting in the regulation of otherwise unregulated markets and the prevention of their misuse.

On the surface, the Bill appears to be very restrictive in nature, as it seeks to prohibit all private crypto currencies, including mining and trading. The Bill also seeks to promote the 'official virtual currency' that will be issued by the Central Govt and the Reserve Bank of India. Furthermore, when compared to similar economic offences, the penalties prescribed by the Bill appeart obedis proportionately harsher. However, the Bill' yet to be made public, and as such, it may differ significantly from the provisions of the previous draught Abolishment of Cryptocurrency and Regulation of Official Digital Currency Bill, 2019.

The question now is whether prohibiting all private VCs and creating a single regulated' of ficial virtual currency' defeats the purpose of Virtual currencies in generalor is justified given the volatility and potential for abuse.

The fact still remains that, just like with any system, there is an inherent risk. Given the benefits of Virtual Currencies, it is possible that regulating rather than banning would have been a better approach. Countries such as Canada regulate VC sunder their anti-money laundering laws[19], trading in Virtual Currencies is authorized on an open exchange, and the income generated is taxed under their income taxlaws[20]. VCs are also used to obtain goods and services. Furthermore, the use of Virtual currencies as payment systems is permitted in Japan.[21]

Crypto trading platforms in India are seeing a significant increase in volume. According to a recentreport[22], WazirX, India's largest crypto currency exchange, recorded an annual trade of more than $43 Billion. If regulated properly, the government can tax the revenue generated, that can benefit both the governmentandthe investors.

While there are legitimate concerns about the use of venture capital, regulation rather than prohibition may be a more viable option in India, and embracing venture capital may have served as a way for India to direct the way intothe future.

CHAPTER SEVEN

Conclusion

Observing the conditions of the other countries, the authors reached on the conclusion that there should not be complete ban on crypto currencies in India. Government should make the laws to regulate crypto currencies in the country.

Printed by Libri Plureos GmbH in Hamburg,
Germany